Salvation of the True Rock

The Sufi Poetry of Najat Ozkaya

Translated and Introduced
by John R. Mabry

the apocryphile press
BERKELEY, CA
www.apocryphile.org

apocryphile press
BERKELEY, CA

Apocryphile Press
1700 Shattuck Ave #81
Berkeley, CA 94709
www.apocryphile.org

Printed in the United States of America
ISBN 978-1-937002-09-1

Salvation of the True Rock

The Sufi Poetry of Najat Ozkaya

Contents

Introduction

I had long wanted to visit Konya, the famed city of Rumi, but as it happened I went there largely by accident. I went to assist a friend with his research on Shams Tebrizi, and along the way largely abandoned that well-intentioned pursuit (sorry, Ian!) after running afoul of another Sufi troublemaker, Najat Ozkaya.

We were in the tiny, dusty library of the Bu Bir Şaka mosque, which must have been a sleepy village mosque in the 14th century when Najat was writing. The mosque itself dates back to the 12th century, full of rough-hewn charm and threadbare carpet. Today, the mosque sits in a residential neighborhood filled with the noise of scooters, the distant sound of an oud blaring from overdriven shop speakers, and skinny kittens covered with sores.

We were not having much luck with our research. I had recently added Turkish to my list of academic languages (which means I read it poorly, speak it not at all, and know how to look up absolutely anything) and had learned to recognize Shams' name in Persian and Arabic, as well. I was sorting through a pile of codices with little success and less hope. It was stinking hot, and Ian, bless him, is one of those academic types who only remembers to bathe sporadically.

One morning I happened upon a 16th century anthology of Sufi poetry, compiled by Lâmiî Çelebi of Bursa and titled, *Ruh Soluyor* (*Gasping of the Soul*). Intrigued, I snapped about a hundred pages with my iPhone and in my spare time began to haltingly decipher its contents.

I have always enjoyed Sufi poetry. Part of the reason I agreed to help Ian is that I am, in fact, a sizeable fan of Rumi, as well as Yunus Emre, Hafiz, and others. I came to Konya as much to help my friend as to pay my respects at Rumi's tomb (and, of course, Shams'). I was delighted to see what poems a 16th century compiler would select, and there were indeed some great ones. But my favorites were two by a poet I had never heard of: Najat Ozkaya.

The next day I had Najat on the brain, and while Ian took a cigarette break in the courtyard of the mosque, I went back over the materials we had already sorted through. And that's when I found it: a Najat stash.

Najat's Works

It wasn't all in one place, nor was it complete. According to the compiler of the anthology, Najat is the author of five works, "Discourses on Ultimate Things," "Sermons to the Damned," "Tail of the Donkey," "A Soul of Beaten Felt," and "The Absence of Light" the last three of which are collections of poetry.

Further research turned up an incomplete copy of "A Soul of Beaten Felt" at the Aziziye mosque, and a complete copy at the Selimiye mosque, also in Konya. I found another complete copy, useful for comparison, in the library of a Sufi madrassah in nearby Karaman. There I also found a complete copy of "The Absence of Light" and several poems from "Tail of the Donkey" in other anthologies. I have not yet been successful at locating either his sermons or his discourses.

Najat's collections do not seem to cohere to any discernable structure. The arrangement seems to be random and the collections, despite their evocative titles, do not seem to be in any way thematic. Consequently, I have felt free to follow my own instincts as to what to include in this collection, and indeed, all three of his poetic collections are represented (although, admittedly, "Tail of the Donkey" only has one representative in this volume).

A more scholarly presentation would include the complete collections, in order, with annotations, and indeed, such an edition of "The Absence of Light" is underway. But the purpose of this collection is not academic, but spiritual enjoyment. I hope that the many readers of Coleman Barks' "translations" of Rumi might discover in Najat some of that same irreverent reverence, that luminosity for which the Mevlana is famous. This edition, then is intended as an introduction for everyday people—folks like you and me, really, who love Rumi and want more of him.

Comparisons to Rumi

Najat is not Rumi, of course, but they have many things in common. For one thing, both had Sufi teachers for their fathers, and both became teachers in their own right, although Rumi was by far a more public figure. Najat ran no school and founded no order, instead he mentored individuals who (his poetry seems to suggest) just "showed up" and asked to be instructed.

Both lived in Konya, but while Rumi was an immigrant from what we now call Afghanistan, Najat was a local. Both were Sufis, but only Rumi's order spins—we do not know Najat's lineage, but he never mentions *sema* (spinning as a form of prayer), so it is safe to assume he was not a Mevlani (a member of Rumi's order).

Other similarities between them concern the poetry itself. While Rumi wrote in Persian, Najat wrote in his own late medieval Turkish vernacular. Yet both are concerned with the relationship between the soul and Allah (and the ultimate identity of one with the other). Both are free-thinkers, their language seeming often scandalous, blasphemous, or, at times, cryptic. They are both humorous at times (and know it) and an earnest playfulness is evident in the writings of both poets. Najat, however, is less overtly devotional than Rumi. He plays his divine love affair closer to the caftan, so to speak. He can gush, at times, but his is not the geyser that Rumi is.

Najat's relationship with the Beloved seems more contentious, sometimes angry or resentful, at turns tentative and abandoned. But for all his vicissitudes, he is always sincere. Because of this, he gives us something unique that, while present in other poets, is far more pronounced in Najat's writing: a transgressive, critical approach to faith that is both questioning and embracing at the same time.

One more similarity with Rumi is worth noting: the quality of their poems is wildly uneven. For that reason alone, it seemed wise to collect my favorites among Najat's verse instead of doing a "complete" edition, since some of the poems would tax even the most eager readers of Sufi poetry.

It seems sad to me that Najat's work has been largely forgotten, while Rumi's is so widely and universally celebrated. Certianly, Rumi is the superior poet, but it is my hope that Najat, even being, as he is, a lesser light, may yet have another opportunity to shine, even if this time around his audience is a people he would not have been able to even conceive of.

Najat's Style

Najat's favored poetic form is the three line stanza, which is his own innovation and virtually unknown in other Turkish poetry. I have tried to preserve this form where I can, but often where the concision of Turkish allows for three lines, the cumbersomeness of English requires four in order to communicate the same sense of the verse. No doubt this is due to my own limitations as a poet and translator, and I beg the reader's indulgence to whatever violence I have done to Najat's intended form.

Najat's tone is more formal than what you see here, and partly it is because he is conforming to poetic norms of his own time. Yet despite this, his playfulness, aggression, and irreverence shine through. Instead of a literal translation, I have followed the lead of Coleman Barks and Daniel Ladinsky's renderings of Hafiz, and given Najat's words a 21st century poetic gloss that, if I am successful, captures the same balance of contemporary "presence" that these wonderful translators have achieved. My hope is to make the work accessible to contemporary audiences, while still preserving Najat's intended meaning.

This has sometimes necessitated some "creative" renderings. For instance, "ass in the air" in the Poem "Surrender" is a rather free translation of "kalça yükseltmek" which, literally rendered, is "raise your hips." In another poem, "Not Speaking" I render the curious Turkish phrase "karanlık kalça" (literally, "dark hips") as "round brown behind," which seems to be congruent with the basic tone of the poem.

The word "snuggle" in "What You Were Made For" is my interpretation of "dayanacak şekilde," "to rest against." "Scrunch" in "Down from Heaven," just sounded more evocative to me than "press," ("basın"). One example that works equally well, or perhaps better, in the original is the word "nişanlanma" in the poem "Commitment." I have rendered the word "commitment," but it actually means, "betrothal."

One more example: I render "Allah's embrace can lead one— kicking and screaming—to Heaven or to Hell." "Kicking and screaming" are my words: Najat's word is borrowed from Arabic: "jihad," which literally means "struggle." It is my belief that Najat's meaning would have gotten lost had I also borrowed that very loaded Arabic word.

Other possible examples are numerous, but these should suffice.

Titles & Arrangement

Najat did not title his poems. All the titles are mine, and I apologize if this misrepresents him. Barks and Ladinsky have done the same with Rumi and Hafiz, respectively, so if I am guilty, I am at least condemned in fitting company.

As far as arrangement of the poems go, I have attempted to mimic Najat's own lack of concern for thematic arrangement by honoring randomness. I have done this by titling all the poems, and then arranging the poems afterwards in alphabetical order, in much the same manner as I have done in the collections of my own poetry, *Sponge Racing and the Way of the World,* and *Gad! The Fish are Chirping.*

Najat scholarship is, of course, in its infancy. I feel deeply privileged to have stumbled upon him, and I hope that you will feel some of the same affinity for his work that I have. Najat speaks something that we rarely hear in religious discourse: friendly opposition. Often, that opposition is interior to himself, which makes Najat's work refreshing, soulful, and complex.

John R. Mabry
Konya, Turkey
8/13/11

Salvation of the True Rock

Süleymaniye Mosque, Istanbul, Turkey

Absolute Submission

Ali the Baker is wringing his hands,
agonizing over a decision.
I wonder if he has prayed about it, and ask
"And what does Allah say about this?"
Whereupon he looks at me as if I have turned into hummus.

I find it curious
that so many people profess to be Muslims
who have no actual acquaintance with Allah.
It's a bit like a man who brags about his diet
but never actually puts anything in his mouth.

Listen to Najat: Allah doesn't want your allegiance,
He wants your heart. He wants to share in your life.
He wants to cry with you when you grieve,
agonize and discern with you at your crossroads,
celebrate with you when you succeed.

Allah has given us so much,
why do we share so little with Him?
The prophet—peace be upon him—
insisted on absolute submission to Allah.
Do you dare to offer Him crumbs?

Allah Cannot Be Caged

Some people think that if they are diligent in their prayer
and observant in their spiritual practice
that Allah will behave Himself
and do whatever they ask of Him.

Religion is a good and noble thing
and being observant is helpful indeed
but such people are mistaken if they think
that Allah is so easily caged or controlled.

Tragedy does not care how religious you are.
A sandstorm will blow over the Sultan's tent
just as quickly as the herdsman's.

If you want to be successful, work hard.
If you want to be loved, pray.

Trust Najat on this:
When you are loved,
hardship is so much easier to bear.

Allah Needs You

I'm sorry I made you angry.
You were telling me about how things should be
and about how Allah should not allow this and that

and instead of agreeing with you
I smiled.

I meant no offense.
Please don't leave the café,
please don't deprive us of your company.

We need you at the mosque.
So please, stick around.
Allah needs you to tell Him how things ought to be done.

Göreme, Cappadocia, Turkey

Allah, the Merciful

The Holy Book says Allah is merciful.
The word of the Prophet—peace be upon him—is always true
so I affirm this as an article of our faith.

Still, I wonder about this "mercy" thing.
I know my Beloved pretty well, and just between you and me,
I have never seen an occasion that requires it of Him.

I have never seen Allah angry
(although I have been angry with *Him* many times).
I have never seen Allah jealous,
nor vengeful, nor cruel, nor punishing.
I have never seen Allah force anyone to cower before Him,
pleading for her life.

So why all this talk of mercy?

Listen to Najat: Lovers forgive.
Mercy is only required
of gods unworthy of your worship.

Allah's Help

Today I am sick and my Beloved offers to make soup
  until I am better.
I do not want soup.
I want to be well.

I tell Him this and He laughs at me
and offers to fluff my pillow.
He asks me if I need another blanket.

I ask Him if perhaps I need another God
who will not be so reluctant to use His power
in a way that will actually be useful.

He says I am cranky
and when my headache goes away
I will feel better and will remember how to be kind.

I want to punch Him in the nose
but I am too weak,
so I lay there thinking of rude retorts.

"If you really loved me," I say,
"you would take this illness from me
and restore me to my power, so that I might
praise you with a whole heart and serve you with vigor."

He smiles and says, "I don't need to prove my love for you,
you don't need to be powerful,
and you don't serve me with vigor even when you're well."

I feel ashamed and realize I'm not fooling anyone.
So I roll in my blankets, and blow my nose
and drink his tea gratefully.

Listen, Najat knows how frustrating life can be
when we have no control over things
and Allah will do nothing to help us.

My only consolation is in comparing myself
to those who are *really* suffering.
and have no voice of their own.

So if you want to complain to Allah about something,
if you want to protest His inaction, or His lack of care,
complain for them.

Whining about yourself will get you nowhere.

Ambition

Have I done enough?
This question whips at my soul like the Sirocco
and leaves me restless and dissatisfied with my lot.

What is this restless ambition that plagues my soul?
Have I not done all that I have done for the Beloved?
And have I not been blessed with true friends and soulful labor?

Would I trade a humble and true treasure
for an empty dream of fame and wealth?
Am I a such a fool?

Winds pass.
I will stay planted like this palm and withstand them.
Allah, my Love, be merciful, and bring me water.

Are You Sure About This?

Are you sure about this?
You could pick anyone as your lover.

You could have picked someone who was
much more beautiful than I am
much holier than I am
much more talented
more articulate than I

You could have picked someone
far less likely to put his foot in his mouth
less adept at making stupid mistakes
someone with a lick of sense

You could have picked someone obedient
someone who didn't argue with you over everything
someone who will do as you ask and not question you
someone *decent*

So I guess I just don't get it
—why this interest in *me*?
You could have done so much better.

Najat says: Shush, dear, be easy.
You're the only God I know
and the only God I *want* to know.
Of course I would have picked *you*.

Commitment

Yesterday a seeker came to me
all excited about Allah
and wanting the advice of an experienced dervish.

When I asked him if he liked kissing
he threw a chair at my head
   and said he had heard about people like me.
So I thought, "I must not be so vague
   or he will misunderstand me."

So I asked him how it felt to be ravished by Allah
to have His kisses covering your neck until dawn,
and the man looked at me with genuine terror.

"Look," I told the man, "what is it you want out of prayer?"
He scratched at his head and looked at his feet.
I tried again,
   "What do you think Allah wants from your prayer?"

Again, he said nothing, but looked a bit like a schoolboy
afraid to give a wrong answer.
I sighed and silently set about making tea.

Truly, I am not a very good dervish.
Allah and I have been lovers so long
that sometimes I forget that there are people
who don't know how to kiss.

I poured him some tea, and gave him a compassionate look.
"Has there ever been a time when a young girl in your village
decided you were the man she wanted to marry?"

He smiled faintly and nodded. "More than once," he said.
I nodded. "Those girls are just like Allah,
Their hearts are set, and there's no talking them out of it."

I told him, "So you have a choice:
You can either start a proper courtship,
or you can let Him down easy,
and speak to Him now and again with kindness,
or you can be a bastard and break His heart."

The man looked at me as if he were staring at his executioner.
Then without a word he picked up his satchel and left.
My wife came in and began to clear the teacups.

"Beginner?" she asked.
I nodded.
"Men are always afraid of commitment," she said.
I smiled.

Connection

This evening I sat at the bedside of old Ali,
his voice as dry as sand,
his eyes searching yet unseeing.

I listened as he recounted his genealogy
from ancient times to the present
from Abraham—peace be upon him—
to his own father in one unbroken line.

I listened in awe as the generations he summoned
transported us swiftly through the years
and ending with his own great-grandson Ishmael.

You might have thought it was boring, but it wasn't.
Some people will admit that
   they find the mosque services boring,
so people are just people and you can't judge them too harshly.

But truly, I found Ali's genealogy
   and the services at the mosque
fascinating for precisely the same reason:
both were acts of worship.

An old dervish I know once told me that
worship is any act that connects us to the larger Reality
of which we are so small a part. He was wise.

I love the prayers, because when I kiss the ground,
it connects me to all the men and women
who have prayed these words before.

I love my religion, because it connects me
to all those who have followed it in the past,
and all those who will follow it in the future.

I love the hajj, because when I walk it
I am connected to all those
   who have walked its dusty roads before me,
and all those who *will* walk it.

I love those moments when a dribble of sadness
   erupts from my throat unbidden
or a shout of joy bubbles up unforeseen
for these connect me with my Beloved.

And here is Ali, speaking the connection between himself
   and the prophet Abraham—peace be upon him—
like the words of the Friday liturgy,
spoken with as much reverence and authority
   as any imam has ever spoken.

The Corpse

The city is buzzing this morning.
A corpse was found just outside the gate.
I join the crowd of onlookers as the watchmen examine him.
My heart sinks into my bowels—I know him.

Perhaps he died trying to get in
before the chill east wind took him.
More likely his heart burst from love unrequited.

I don't go closer.
I fear, for I am complicit in this crime.
I do not need to see the face to know who it is.
It is Allah.
But I'll end up as cold and stiff as he is
if I say so
aloud.

Courage

Your fear is not my concern.
Your fear is a wall that needs to be burst through
without regard for your comfort or your feelings.

Sorry to be so harsh, but that's the way it is.
These things cannot be handled by feathers or soft gloves.
They need hammers and chisels and oxen
pulling with all their strength.

Allah's day is short
and your time here is uncertain
and there is so much to be done.

We have to pull down this whole structure
so that we can begin to build again
and there is no gentle way to do that.

Listen to Najat, my friend,
for this is the only kindness you will receive.
Grit your teeth and sieze your courage
from the nafs that threaten to steal it from you.

Demolition is mandatory.
Fear is normal, courage is optional
but highly recommended.

Courage is also a gift from Allah
that is yours for the asking.
Why are you not on your knees yet?

Dangerous Faithfulness

I have left the café tonight
mad as a hornet
having listened for far too long
to proud men boasting about their piety.

I cannot bear to hear another travelogue of the hajj
or of how Allah has blessed them with riches,
while I know for a fact that their own neighbors
went to bed tonight with bellies strangled from want.

They will not heed my warning, however.
If I protest they will mock me and turn me out into the street.
After all, what am I but a foolish dervish?

But because Najat has read the Holy Qur'an,
and has treasured its wisdom in his heart,
he knows this for certain:

Righteousness such as theirs is a growing stockpile of coal
that they will carry with them into Hell.
Even Iblis was banished for his faithfulness.

Translator's Note: Iblis is the name given to Satan in the Qur'an. When Allah cre-
ated Adam, he commanded all the angels to bow down and worship the first
man. Iblis refused to worship any but Allah, and was cast out for his disobedience.

The Desert

In this desert, I see no life.
No creature scurries,
no sign of green creeps across this landscape.

Yet my Beloved has lured me out here and abandoned me.
And it's not the first time, either.
Remind me, why should I not be upset about this?

My mind waxes philosophical
and insists that there are things to be learned in the desert.
But knowledge is the last thing I am thirsty for, here.

You know what I really want?
Distraction. Because the sameness of the sand and scrub
depress me and distress my spirit.

I want to be anywhere but here.
I want to feel my Beloved again.
I want, I want, I want, I want.

Oh. Okay. I guess there *are* things
to be learned in the desert.
I am breathing. It is enough.

Najat can really be an idiot.

Sit, Najat. Stare at the sand.
And let the emptiness suck the last drop of
triviality and self-obsessed foolishness from your soul.

Discernment

Many times I have asked my Love for guidance.
I plead until my voice is hoarse, but He does not answer.
I cry until my head hurts, but still He does not answer.

I prostrate myself towards Mecca
  and grind my question into the dust before my face.
There is no answer.
I tear at my tunic until I am wearing nothing but threads.
No answer.

This is typical.
If there is one thing Najat has noticed, it is this:
when you want information, Allah is not chatty.

Last night my entreaties went on until morning,
and I fell into an exhausted heap.
As I watched, a raven hopped right up to me,
an olive stuck in his beak,
and cocked his head so that he fixed me with one black eye.
Then he cawed, and flew away.

Najat wants to know: *That's* an answer?

Distress

Be quiet, my soul, no need for all this distress.
Yes, it is true, yesterday you were unfaithful.
Allah was not the object of your desire.

Lucky for you, though, Allah does not hold grudges.
This day's sun is new, and dew has washed clean
the dust from every leaf and stone.

This day I will choose my Love more wisely.
This day I will reserve my affection
for Him who is worthy of it.

We all do this, of course.
Every day we choose whom we will love.
Every day we choose the lips that will touch our own.

Beloved, forgive me.
Your servant Najat is a careless fool.
This day when I prostrate myself toward Mecca
I will not be thinking
of something else.

Don't Feel Bad

Don't feel bad.
You were not made for days like this.
You were made for days that are wild with passion
and for nights hot with wine and sweat and kisses
and the whispering of secrets.

But *this* day is a day of longing
of crying out into empty air, "Where are you?"
When your Love is nowhere to be seen,
and the waiting seems worse than death.

"Why," you cry, "has my Love abandoned me?
Did I not dote enough?
Were there not enough tender words?
Or too many spoken in anger?"

Najat says, Shush. Don't feel bad. Days end.
Your love has never stopped caressing you,
and covers your neck with kisses even as you hear these words.
That you do not feel Him with you all the time is no one's fault.
You *must* turn your face away from Him
or His brilliance will make you blind.

Don't Think You Are Special

Allah is surprisingly undiscriminating
regarding those upon whom He chooses
  to shower His affection.
Just look at me
—a rogue of suspect reputation and meager means—
and yet I have been bathed in His kisses
and clothed in His everlasting kindness.

Don't think you are special. You aren't.
I don't care you who are
I don't care what you've done
I don't care who you've hurt
or what blasphemies you have uttered.
Nothing in your history could possibly be so notorious
that it would deter His relentless pursuit of your heart.

I have been Allah's lover for years now
and I can tell you two things about Him with absolute certainty:
no prostitute is more careless with her affections
and no hunter more stubborn in pursuit of his prey.

Listen to Najat: When you realize He has his heart set on you
just give up and surrender to His seduction,
or you will be running from His advances
until you lay down in the grave
with Him.

Down from Heaven

The imams say that the Christians will be chastised
　by Allah on the Day of Judgment
for preaching that the prophet Jesus
—peace be upon him—is Allah in human form.

I say that the Christians err only in saying
that the prophet Jesus alone
is the incarnation of Allah.

For if all this wide world is illusion
except for the Beloved,
then every child is sent from Allah, and is Allah.

For only in Him do we have any ground to stand on
any reality to boast of
any substance one can touch.

There is no light in our eyes but His.
There is no nose to scrunch that is not, ultimately, His nose.
There is no giggle or cry that is not an expression of His Voice.

There is no sin in saying,
"This baby has come down from Heaven,"
for truly, what child hasn't?

A Drop of Pain

I do not deny that there is great suffering in this world.
And what kind of Muslim would I be if I did not believe
that Allah had the power to subdue it?

Why He does not subdue it
when so many good and innocent people suffer
is a great mystery that I have not yet divined.

What I do know is this: that for every drop of pain,
there is an ocean of joy
and that I would not know one without the other.

And that is Allah's gift and Allah's wisdom.

My own widowed mother, as much as I love her
forsakes the ocean and praises the drop
at great length, every time I see her.

Many people do this.
And this, it seems to me,
is an even greater mystery.

Drunkenness and Wine

When merchants visit Christian lands
they often find it difficult
to refuse the wine.

They tell me it is heavenly, soft as a sunset
a warm blanket pulled over the mind
and gladsome to the heart.

I never touch the stuff.
I've been to Christian lands
and "no" is the easiest word to utter.

Listen to Najat: Wine isn't hard to refuse
but drunkenness should call upon you
daily.

Ottoman house, Safranbolu, Turkey

Faith and Belief

You do not say, "I have faith that I lay with my wife last night."
You know whether you did or not,
   and faith does not enter into it.

You do not say, "I believe I have eaten."
You know whether your belly is growling or if it is satisfied.
What need is there to speak of "belief"?

The religious man is all about "faith" and "belief,"
but I have about as much use for these things as I do bedbugs.

"Faith" and "belief" are a plague upon the Ummah.
"Faith" is playing make believe
   until something real comes along.
"Belief" is an opinion that you cannot prove,
 yet you will not hesitate to kill to defend.

This is madness.

Listen to Najat:
When Allah, touches your soul, you will know it.
When Allah takes you in a fit of passion, you will know it.
When Allah seizes your spirit and makes you His own,
   you will know it.

When Allah tenderly caresses your skin,
covers your mouth with kisses,
and longingly calls your name all night over the desert,
   you will know it.

Words like "faith" or "belief"
will not suggest themselves to your use
any more than dung will suggest itself for dinner.

Fire

Here is a fire that threatens to consume all:
my house, my wife, my children,
my possessions, my goats, my wealth.

Even now the flames lick at my face
and I can see it coming—
the utter destruction of all that I love:

my neighbors, my village, the mosque,
and even more dear,
my body, my life, my identity.

All that I am, all that I have, nothing more than
ashes caught in dust devils
wobbling across wastes of sand.

And you, my Love, you stand by
not with water to douse this conflagration
but with a fan to urge sparks into disaster.

Najat knows you don't mean any harm
—but utter and complete destruction
  of all that I know and love?
Oh, yes. That you most certainly intend.

Five Pillars

The five pillars are not disciplines imposed upon you
by a harsh taskmaster
out of cruelty or spite. Not at all.

Love asks us to proclaim our faith
as a formal answer to a formal question,
"Will you marry me?"

Love asks us to pray five times a day
because any lover longs to express her affection
at least as often.

We give a bit of our plenty to those in need,
because love that is truly received naturally multiplies
and spills out all around.

Love asks us to fast only to remind us
of what it was like before our hearts
were so full.

Love invites us to travel to show us
that He is present with us
everywhere we go.

Listen to Najat: These five practices
are not arduous requirements of our faith.
They are the five fingers on the hand of Love
that draw you in to Allah's embrace.

Five Times a Day

I am lying in the shade near the village well
while old Muhamet's widow scolds,
shaking her fist and calling me "lazy."

She has been a widow for many years now,
so perhaps she has forgotten
  that when you make love for hours on end
you need to rest a bit before you can do it again.

Her shrieking is interrupted by the distant cry of the muezzin,
and with a yawn and a stretch I get to my feet.
My love is calling me for another roll in the hay.

Five times a day is too much for some people.
But Najat knows that when Allah picks you for his lover,
He gives you amazing powers of endurance.

Gift

Allah's embrace can end worlds or begin them.
Allah's embrace can bring hope or despair.
Allah's embrace can lead one
   —kicking and screaming—to Heaven or to Hell.

Allah's embrace can kindle resentment or affection.
Allah's embrace can bring clarity or madness.
Allah's embrace can snuff out your life or redeem it.

And the mystery of it is that these opposites
—life and death, sadness and joy, suffering and grace—
are always performed with one and the same act.

How you perceive it is largely determined
by the posture of your hand:
is it open to receive, or is it balled into a fist?

Najat knows life can be hard.
I've seen my share of blessings wrapped in pain.
I, too, struggle to behold all that Allah gives as a gift.

Gratitude

On days that are dark
When windstorms hide the sun
From the eyes of my heart
When Allah feels far and a stranger to me

That's when my soul says to me,
"get up you worthless clot of blood
  and go in search of gratitude."
You see, I have much experience with wind-storm days
and I know that if I can find enough gratitude
to balance the weight of a grain of sand
I can redeem the day.

On days when I find it
I enshrine it in the Kabaa of my heart
I circle it seven times
and then I go home
restored to my Beloved.

This pilgrimage
which has been my salvation many times
can be completed in about the time it takes
to boil an egg.

On days when I nurture my separation
like a sullen child's pout
I can give no excuse
for not taking the little Hajj.
That is when I must trust that Allah
Will come and search for me
In the sandstorm.

Invariably, when He finds me
He shakes his head and gives me a playful slap.
"You could not be bothered to find a grain of sand,"
He says, with a note of sadness in his throat,
"Even when it is blowing all around you."

Listen to Najat,
If you cannot see gratitude swirling about you
It is because you are deliberately shutting your eyes,
Stuffing up your ears, and holding closed your nose and mouth.
You can die like that, you know.

Hard to Get

The morning sky shrieks light and cries, "I am in love with you!"
The rooster answers but I hunker down in my blankets
and try to ignore it.

At midday the sun blazes away screaming,
  "Come away with me!"
But I seek out the shade
and stuff bread in my ears.

At night the stars sing faintly and sweetly, "Make love to me!"
But I am throwing dice and drinking coffee with my friends
and although I hear them, I pretend that I do not.

In my dream the Beloved punches me in the face and says,
"Why are you playing hard to get?"
In my dream, Najat says nothing.

How Lovers Long to Die

Once, when I was exploring the ruins of an ancient palace,
I sat beneath the shade of a date tree
to eat the meal I had packed.

Soon after I had finished, as I sat enjoying the breeze
a doe approached me, her muzzle gray
and her movements stiff with age.

Fearing I would frighten her, I tried not to move.
In wonder I watched as she sniffed at my hand,
then stumbled, sank to her knees,
  and gently laid her head in my lap.

One black eye met mine,
Then light within it faded,
And she was dead.

This is how lovers long to die,
at the end of many fine years,
their faces caressed by the hands of Love as the light fades
from their eyes.

Najat says, You do not need to wait
until the hour of your death
to rest your head in the lap of your Beloved.

How to Grow Your Soul

Here you are,
knocking at my door,
drinking my tea
and asking me how to grow your soul.

And yet, when I say you must give your money
to the widow down the alley,
you make excuses.

When I say you must be diligent in your prayers,
You wave it away, and say, "yes of course, I do them."
But there is no passion in your voice.

When I say you must keep halal,
you roll your eyes as if I were your mother
telling you to clean up after yourself.

I don't know why you came to me.
Did you think I was going to tell you
to do something arcane or secret?

There is no secret to growing your soul.
Every imam knows how to do it.
Every Muslim should.
Every Sufi pretends to, at least.

The prophet did not give us our tradition
because he had nothing better to do.
His revelation cost him dearly, or have you forgotten?

Do you aspire to be a thief in Allah's kitchen?

You knocked on my door, so listen to what Najat has to say:

If you want to go on the hajj,
do not think you can do it
carried aloft on the shoulders of servants
without breaking a sweat.

There are no shortcuts to Mecca.

I Am Not a Believer

Stop with your accusations!
I am not a religious man, and never have been.
I am not attached to anyone's sacred writings,
   or teachers, or mosques.

They are like candied dates:
pleasurable, but not enough to sustain one's life.
They are like the shimmering silks
   worn by a beautiful and seductive woman:
nice, but the real pleasure comes when she takes them off.

So stop calling me "holy man" "teacher" "religious" "believer"
I have as little use for these names
   as I have for a belt made of scorpions.

Married couples do not call each other
   "husband" or "wife" when they are alone.
They just say, "Honey" or "Sweetheart" or "My love"
or, more likely, just "kiss me."

There is a difference between the mind and the heart.
Religions want your mind to be a certain way,
   to believe certain things,
so they can tell if you are "one of us" or "one of them."
They love to name things, define them,
   so they can tell who are the "true believers."

But Najat says, Listen: I am not a believer.
I want to take off the silks and get down to business.
I am not religious.
I am a punch-drunk fool
in love.

If I Had a Servant

If I had a servant,
I would command him to make my tea
and would sit in the shade, and glory in the breeze.

If I had a servant,
she would keep the house clean
and my wife would have time to socialize
  with the other women of means.

If I had a servant,
he would carry my things to and from the madrasah,
leaving my hands empty for hugging and slapping at shoulders.

If I had a servant,
she would cook for us the most amazing meals,
(which is more than my poor wife has ever done).

I thank Allah I do not have a servant,
  for then I would be damned.
And no servant, no matter how loyal,
is going to come and carry my soul out of Hell.

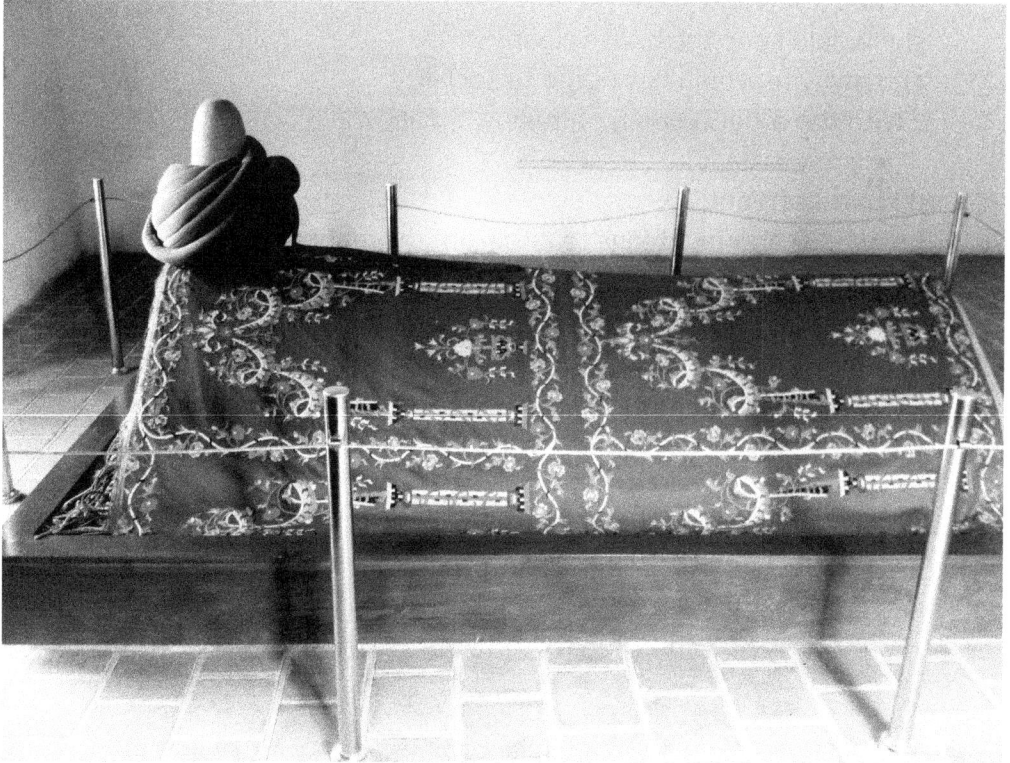

The tomb of Najat Ozkaya, Konya, Turkey.

If You Want to Be Great

Many people want to be great
in the eyes of Allah
but this is impossible.

The powerful are as ants at His feet.
The holy are like grave clothes,
fetid and falling away.

You cannot gain Allah's esteem
by lording power over great cities
or by your righteousness,
no matter how celebrated or by whom.

Real love is not impressed by greatness
but by humility
and sincerity.

If you want Allah's esteem
you must throw yourself at His feet,
admit your darkest secret
howl the awful truth of your soul before His presence
and surrender every hope of greatness.

Listen to Najat:
Allah alone is great.
The best we can hope for is to be embraced
even in our shame.

Imagination

I have no interest in proving to you
that Allah exists, or in persuading you
that His eye and His care are always upon you.

For such things do not fall into the realm of reason,
regardless of what the jurists argue.
This sort of thing involves the imagination and the heart.

I imagine that Allah is there, and He *is* there.
I imagine that Allah cares, and it is clear to me that He does.
I imagine that Allah speaks to me, and His voice is plainly heard.

You are quite right that I might be making it all up,
that Allah is a figment of my imagination.
I find it just as likely, however, that you are a figment of His.

Consider, for a moment, that the imagination
does not conjure up only fantasies, but might in fact
be an organ of perception, like unto the eye or the ear.

Consider, please, the fact that everything
that human beings create must first be imagined
and only then do they take form.

Are songs, stories, buildings, furniture,
clothing, food, or even children imaginary?
And yet all of these things
  were imagined before they took shape.

Allah imagined the world, and it came into being.
Allah imagined you, and you came into being.
It seems to me that you might, at the very least,
   return the favor.

The Intimacy of Silence

I am sitting with this person
who doesn't know how to shut up
and I want to strangle him.

Most people are terrified of silence.
They will chatter on about absolutely nothing
just to avoid it.

It's not that they love the sound of their own voices,
it's that they can't stand the absence,
the quiet, the nothing.

The reason they hate it so, I think,
is that silence is incredibly intimate.
And intimacy scares people.

Listen to Najat:
Words are clothes,
but silence is nakedness.

Prayer is no time for modesty.
If you really want to get close to Allah,
you must not be afraid to get naked with Him.

Thanks to Dan Prechtel for his help with a tricky bit of translation on this one.

—JRM

Topkapi Palace, Isanbul, Turkey

Jesus and the Dog

Once when the prophet Jesus—peace be upon him—
was walking on a dusty and deserted road.
On his way to an urgent engagement
he came upon a dog, who was sick and nearly lifeless.

Moved with compassion, he touched the animal's matted fur.
The dog opened one eye and whined weakly,
then opened its mouth and gave his hand one affectionate lick.

The prophet then cradled the animal in his arms,
and carried him all the way to his destination.
When he arrived, the dog had died.

He instructed some youths to bury the beast in a field
with respect and dignity,
and then set off to his appointment.

When the townsfolk heard what had happened,
they asked him, "Why did you carry a dead dog into our village?
Why did you not leave him on the side of the road
  where you found him?"

As the prophet set out to wash himself, he answered them,
"If I had sat with the dog until he had died,
  I would have missed my engagement.
If I had simply left him there, he would have died alone.

"Allah commands all people to have compassion
  upon even the lowest of beasts.
So I picked him up and carried him until he died
so that he would enter paradise with a friend at his side.

"Be at peace, and do not wonder at this.
For surely, if I have done it for this dog,
I would do it for you."

Just Listen

Quiet!... Damn, now I've lost it.
You have to listen close to hear the whisper of the Beloved.
Can you hear it? No? Have you tried?

To hear this Voice, you do not have to go to any special schools.
No degrees or diplomas will help you here.
If anyone tells you he is an expert, take my advice and run away.

Who knows what voice such a person is listening to,
and whether or not it is from Allah?
Only you can discern that, and you must be silent to do it.

So leave the schools behind you
and tell the teachers to stop their jabbering.
Tell the experts to find other fools
   from whom they can swindle their bread.

Enter the cave of your heart and sit in silence
until the Beloved approaches you from behind
wraps His arms around you,
   and pulls you in to lay against His breast.

Then listen, and listen well.
Remember the words He speaks in those intimate moments
and share them with the world when you have gone out again.

Does it seem strange to share
   such whispered intimacies with strangers?
Is there anything about Allah that is *not* strange?
Is there anything about this dance of the soul
   that does not confound you?

Najat is no expert in anything.
Just ask my wife if you don't believe me.
She will tell you. She is not shy.
Najat has just practiced the art of sinking back
   into the Divine embrace
   and listening.

Don't try to make sense of it.
You can't. Just do it.
You can.

Just So You Know

Just so you know
Allah will keep picking at you
until you either
bleed righteousness
or you tell Him to stop it.

Lashing Out

Today I am so angry at Allah
I wish I could hit Him!
I want to punch Him in the face and pull out His hair
and make Him feel even the smallest portion
  of the pain that I feel today.

So instead I rage at the sky
and throw dust at the sun
and roll in the brambles until I bleed.

And when I have shouted myself hoarse
and cried myself dry
and have worked myself into such a miserable state
  I am shaking

Allah comes up behind me,
places His mouth upon my ear, going, "Shush, my love."
I lash out but only succeed in boxing my own ear.

So then He lays beside me,
  his arm around my chest until it is still
whispering, "Calm yourself, my love.
Why don't you tell me how you really feel."

And this is why I hate Him.
He never takes any of my pain seriously.
Not really.

He shows up and acts as if, no matter how much I am suffering,
everything is going to be all right in the end.
And this only serves to make me angrier.

Najat is no idiot.
He knows that Allah is wise.
He only wishes Allah were not so damned smug.

Lay It Down

Make your case, don't pull your punches.
I can take anything you can dish out
and the Beloved can take more.

I know you've been hurt, abused, betrayed. Who hasn't?
The problem is that you lay it all at Allah's feet
and, guilty by association, at my feet as well.

The fact is, it isn't Allah's fault, what happened to you.
The people who hurt you lied to you.
Allah is nothing like what they told you, and never was.

Listen to Najat, for I know how to fix this.
Take every bit of that hurt, abuse, and betrayal
and lay it at the feet of Allah. But this time, leave it there.

Then go and talk to someone who will tell you the Truth.
Those who carry such heavy burdens are deaf,
but the unburdened have the hearing of angels.

The Loneliness of the Desert

The infidels send their holy men
into the desert to commune with their gods
I don't know who they find out there,
   but I don't think it's Allah.

Out there, Allah is just an idea,
as far above them as the scorching sun,
just as distant, just as helpless to save.

For where there are no people
there are no opportunities
for mercy, or justice, or compassion.

Perhaps they find themselves.
But in my opinion, to find oneself in isolation
is the same as being lost.

Listen to Najat:
Every good thing you have ever received from Allah
was passed on to you by human hands.

Love Doesn't Care

Sometimes Love comes calling
and tells me things that the imams would call heresy.
I try to shut Him up, but it's no good.

Love doesn't care.

He goes on and on about how much He loves so-and-so,
even though I know so-and-so is an infidel
and if I breathe a word of this crazy talk to anyone
    I'd end up in jail.

Love doesn't care.

He wants to make love to total strangers
    and asks me to arrange it
and I have to tell Him that this kind of behavior is frowned upon
by the imams and the widows and even the wives.

Love doesn't care.

He is careless with His affections
and He doesn't give a fig who knows it.
I tell Him He is making trouble for me
    and He waves me away with a laugh.

Love doesn't care.

I tell Him that there are rules about these things.
I tell Him that the imams have everything down to a science.
I tell Him that society would fall apart
    if we let Him have His way.

Love doesn't care.

I swear that He wants to upset people.
I think He wants to turn the village upside down.
I think He actually enjoys scandalizing the faithful.

Listen to Najat, you careless lout:
You can say anything to me, and I'll hold it safe.
But you say it out there and I cannot be held responsible.

Have you no regard for you reputation?
Have you no regard for mine?
Have you no shame?

Ah, that's it.
You really don't,
do you?

Love is a Tiger

Love is a tiger
The rarest of cats, He is the very essence of beauty
He is power, muscles rippling just beneath the skin
He is majesty, carrying the balance of life and death
  in His dread jaws

Love is not predictable
He doubles back when you think you are on His trail
He lies in wait for you,
  silent until the moment of the killing pounce
He will find you no matter how deep into the jungle you flee

Love rules all the worlds
Brings them into being with His roar
Brings them to life with hot breath
Plays with them between His paws

Love is terrible
If you are not frightened, you should be.
But Najat says this to you:
Go to your home, and gather your weapons.
Tigers should be hunted.

Love or Fear?

Just stop it.
I hear you whispering, "Blasphemer"
  whenever I walk by.
And you're wrong.

My love for Allah is real, as real as His is for me.
Ours is a passionate, intense relationship.
Like any real relationship it is messy,
  it has its ups and downs,
  it has days of struggle and nights of murmurs and caresses.

Do I get angry at Him? Of course.
Do I tell Him so?
What kind of relationship would we have if I didn't?

If you cannot share your most intimate secrets with Allah
if you are afraid to be honest with Him about how you feel,
then I feel sad for you, because you do not know Him.
Not really.

Listen to Najat: There is not room in the human heart
for both love and fear.
Pick one.

Majesty

Yesterday, Ismail's wife Ali was accused of adultery.
I don't know if she did it,
  but Ismail has always been a bit of an ass.
That is important, though.

What struck at my heart
was the sight of her
being led away through the souk.

For she did not go with her head hanging,
hiding her face from the crowd,
whimpering and wincing when the widows spit on her.

No. She moved through the souk as if carried on a palanquin,
her head held high, her eyes fixed on some distant horizon
visible only to her.

It was the damndest thing, and I cannot explain it
but she seemed to glow as she moved
and the widows froze with their spittle still on their tongues.

The sight of her face, rigid as stone,
yielding to no emotion, without even a hint of shame,
is burned into my brain and my inner eye cannot look away.

Najat knows now that he has seen Majesty.
It was placed within all creatures by Allah
and blazes forth when it is least expected.

It consumes all pretense, all injustice, all unrighteousness
in its indiscriminating fire, and it has nothing to do
with heredity or wealth or armies or land

or gold
or scepters
or crowns.

Ottoman house, Safranbolu, Turkey

My Life with Allah

When I am having a bad day,
Allah whispers in my ear
"This has a really funny ending."

When I am surrounded by friends,
and I feel like singing until dawn,
Allah leads everyone in a dance.

When Mira comes to my bed
cheerfully demanding that I do my husbandly duty
Allah sits in the corner and plays the baglama.

When my heart is broken and I don't know how I can go on,
Allah holds me close to his breast and says,
"This is happening to me, too."

I have heard that the gods of other peoples
   are aloof and selfish in their desires.
But the Prophet—peace be upon him—has revealed
that the true God is closer to me than the vein in my neck.

I am grateful that He is so intimately involved in my affairs.
But I don't think I am special.
I think I am different from most people, though,
   because I let Him.

My Soul Wants to Fly

Today a bird flew into my house and would not leave.
First, I tried to give him ample opportunity to fly away,
opening the door and windows and waiting patiently.

I am still waiting.

Next, I tried to shoo him out, running at him from behind,
with the open door before him.
Instead he fled sideways beneath the safety of a low table.

After that I tried to lure him out with food,
Leaving a trail of tasty seeds from the table to the door.
He ate a few, then, sated, returned to the shelter of the table.

I have given up. It got cold,
so I closed the door and shuttered the windows.
Then I went to bed.

I do not know why that bird did not want to be free.
Oh! I am so stupid.
There, now I see. I guess I do know, after all.

I hope Allah
will not shutter up the house before
my soul has decided to fly.

Night is Coming

Now
the sky is radiating rose and ochre,
night is even now spreading her gown.

I have the shortness of this hour
to say what must be said,
to reveal what is hidden within me

before darkness shrouds this fleeting life forever.
And I—no surprise—feel frozen in my fear.
No words are coming, no thoughts, no epiphanies.

Night is coming. Allah is waiting.
Have mercy, Beloved,
may you deem the desert of my distress a fitting gift.

For I have
nothing else of value to offer
now.

No Help at All

My Beloved is no help at all.

I ask for a needle, He hands me a chicken.
I ask for a hammer, He gives me a bucket.
I ask Him for cloth, He gives me grapes.

Crazy.
This is no way
to run a partnership!

I ask Him for answers, and He gives me a handful of date pits.
I ask Him for comfort, and He shows me a bruise on His elbow.
I ask Him for a display of righteous wrath, and what does He do?
He ignores my enemies and smothers me with kisses.

I would talk to Him
but talking does no good.
He will insist that I sing or dance my complaint
and that will drain it of every last drop of irritation.
Pointless and silly.

Najat knows how to answer this: Ask for nothing
and build a life from the random gifts
that Allah is always sending.

No Shame

I hear your protest, my soul—
the promises you've broken, the loves you've betrayed
the ragged disappointment you've left in your erratic wake.

The Beloved hears you, too
and is deaf to your accusations.
You did what you did
not from pettiness or spite or malevolence,
but from a misdirected desire to be fully embraced.

So hear the wisdom of a deeper voice, now:
Calm yourself, and rest against the bosom of the Beloved.
Let Him kiss the top of your head,
and caress your neck as He rocks back and forth.

This night there is no banishment,
no reprimand,
no punishment,
no shame.

Nor shall there be tomorrow.

No Trick

This is no trick, you know.
Allah does not spend His time contriving
new ways to trip you up.

That is the way of the jinn,
not the way of the Beloved.
For the path that Allah lays out is sincerity itself.

The road to Mecca is straight.
There's really no way to get lost.
Not even fools can go astray, even if they try.

So if you are tired of chasing your tail
if you are lost and despair of finding your way
if you have received confusing directions

come with Najat.
I will take you to the road. I will point the way,
and will walk with you until you are sure of it.

Untold millions have walked it before you,
  so you cannot miss the trail.
And unless they have all been wrong,
you will find what you seek at its end.

Not Speaking

Allah and I are not speaking today. I am angry
—don't ask why, I don't want to go into it with you—
but Allah is bemused and just waiting it out.

An apology would be nice,
but I'm not going to hold my breath.
Allah says He will love me even if I *have* turned blue.

I don't want Him trying to make it up to me, either,
with his cooings and ear-nibblings—
sure I love that stuff, but not when I'm so mad I could spit.

I just want Him to imagine how I must feel for a second,
to understand how cruel and vicious life can be
  when you're not the one holding all the power,
and something like….like *this* happens.

He seems oblivious, though,
and just wants me to sit down, have some tea
and "relax, relax, relax."

Listen to Najat, buster:

If you want to kiss, here's my round brown behind.
I'll "relax" when the energy you put into sympathy
rivals the effort you put into seduction.

Not Tonight

You said, "Make love with me"
and I said, "I don't feel like it tonight"
and now I feel like a heel.

Have you ever said "no" to me?
As far back as I can remember
You have responded to every come-hither look
I ever gave You.

Be patient with me, my Love
and remember the frailty of flesh,
the fickleness of emotion,
and the way every stray breeze
causes my spirit to flicker.

"Not tonight" doesn't mean "go away"
it means please wait for me to come back.

Süleymaniye Mosque, Istanbul, Turkey

One Great Sun

The spiritual life is a purging, an ongoing discernment
between what I am clutching to greedily,
and what I have truly surrendered.

I must constantly be asking myself,
regarding all that I put my hand to,
"Have I surrendered it? Is this under submission to Allah?"

For anything that is not submitted
is a barrier between my Beloved and me.
Anything I clutch as my own steals my heart
  from the One who truly owns it.

I know what you are thinking,
but believe Najat when he says
that this is not tyranny.

This is the hard work of seeing.
This is the sorting of what is Real and what is not.
This is the hard work of putting my soul in order.

The only thing that is Real is Allah.
All other things are shadows cast
by that One Great Sun.

What value are shadows?
And why should I spend my soul
to hide it away like some secret treasure only I may enjoy.

It is no treasure. Not my money, not my house,
not my children, not my wife, not my widowed mother,
not my teachings, not the mosque—not you, my friend.

We are all shadows,
and not one of us has worth apart from Allah.
If that Sun were to stop shining, all of us shadows
  would disappear into black.

I clutch to nothing,
because all but my Beloved *is* nothing.
If I do not see that, I live in illusion.

Therefore everything must be surrendered.
And when I do, it is given back to me,
But I know it for what it is.

This is my religion. Islam means "submission."
If I refuse to submit any one thing,
then I am a hypocrite, or I am deluded, or I am a heretic.

I submit. I surrender.
Allah help me to see
what I have not yet surrendered.

Outward Forms

I understand why, among our people,
  everyone must practice Islam.
Without it, society would once again descend into the chaos
of blood feuds and lawlessness.

What I don't understand is why,
if a man must practice the outward forms of a religion,
he does not avail himself of the inner rewards as well.

It is as foolish as a starving man,
who, when given walnuts, keeps the shells in a bag
and throws the nut meat into the street.

Allah has set before us a grand way of living,
a great feast to nourish and enrich our souls.
Is it not rude to refuse His hospitality?

Parlor Tricks

Last month I saw some Christian priests in Tyre
  making magic bread from ordinary loaves.
Yesterday I saw an Imam in the souk
casting out demons with a talisman.

I have heard of people with many gods
  rolling on the ground and prophesying.
And I think these are all very impressive.
But I do not think I shall do any of these things.

Parlor tricks are all very well and good.
But Najat prefers necking.

The Perfection of Allah

Today I met a man who went on and on
  about the perfection of Allah.
How He is the Highest, the Immutable, the Unattainable.
He waxed poetic in his descriptions,
rapturously describing something beyond conception,
  something untouchable.

I don't know who this man is in love with,
but it certainly doesn't sound like Allah to me.

The Allah I know is not elevated beyond this earth,
but bunched up in the clods I kick on the way to work.
The Allah I love is not perfect,
but a stubborn, difficult, argumentative pain in the ass.
The Allah that kisses my lips as I kneel in prayer,
is not unattainable, but threatens to crush me
  with His embrace.

Immutable? I don't even know what that means.
I'm going to guess it means unemotional,
but my Love is so passionate that I have to push Him away
for fear He will smother me with his kisses
  every time I turn toward Mecca.

Najat says: Don't speak to me about the "perfection of Allah."
Worshipping deities that you dream up yourself
  is called "idolatry."
If you want to know Allah,
  be prepared for the mess He leaves in His wake.

Pleasing Two Loves

It is not easy to find a woman
  who understands my love for Allah.
Some are jealous,
  some want to come first,
  some simply don't understand the attraction.
Pleasing two loves is no sport for the faint of heart.
Ask Malik how peaceful his household is with his two wives,
  or the Sultan with forty-five!

Najat says, if you find a woman
willing to engage in a threesome,
marry her quickly.

The Power of Death

Last night I dreamt I was sitting at the fountain
in the middle of the souk watching the people
as they shopped, gossiped, and milled about.

As I watched, a tiger the size of a large man
slunk silently into the midst of the market
wary of eye and licking his lips.

It seemed that no one saw him but me.
Oblivious, people laughed and argued and haggled
all the while the Power of Death padded at their heels.

Listen, my soul, this is how it is:
the Power of Death is always at our heels,
creeping up behind us, as we go about our business
without a thought for our peril.

Najat has seen him now, and knows that this is no dream.
Those jaws are real, and only the goodness of the Beloved
keeps that cat from catching us before our time.

Preparing the Heart

The body acts.
The mind thinks.
The heart loves.

Allah shaped the body,
Allah inspires the mind,
but it is in the heart that Allah makes His home.

All sensible people love the body
and care for it
as one does one's own house.

An untrained mind
will believe anything
and may betray you.

But—and I think this incredible—
many people neglect the heart,
as if it were not a necessary organ.

Listen to Najat: if you have not prepared your heart,
if you have not learned to love
  even those things you do not love,
you are not yet prepared to welcome the Beloved.

The Promise of Allah

I know you have suffered.
Be at peace.

I know you are angry and confused.
Be still.

I know you are not thinking,
but lashing out in grief and desperation.
Calm your heart.

Listen to the promise of Allah:

The earth has died,
and lies frozen and lifeless.
But life will return to this world.

Your grief has blocked out the sun,
and blinded your spirit.
But color and light will return to your eyes.

Our throats are parched from crying out to Allah,
and the desert has crept into our bellies.
But we will drink once more of salvation,
and have our fill of peace.

If you cannot yet trust Allah, trust Najat.
I have been parched. I have been blind. I have been dead.
I have journeyed to Hell on my flea-bitten donkey and returned.
Allah does not leave His friends to die in the dust.

The Promise of Rain

In the alley I can hear Ahmet screaming at his servants.
The merchant is unhappy because a deal has fallen through
and he must find someone to punish.
Usually, he punishes someone who would sell an arm
  to know a fraction of Ahmet's good fortune in this world.

Above me, the sky grows dark and thunder rolls in the distance.
The dogs in the alley sniff at the wind.
Listen to Najat: These dogs know how it is.
Allah never threatens rain.
He promises it.

Pure Religion

Allah dances like a drunken fool
to the music of the tambur and oud.
He staggers, He laughs, He sways, He falls.

Last week Allah fell into my mind
and I saw visions of the faithful and the damned.
It frightened and inspired me
  and I became more disciplined in my practice.

A couple of days later Allah fell into my limbs
and I felt the strength of tigers.
I put it to good use digging a new well for old Dede.

Then, Allah fell into my throat and I sang like a sparrow
until my wife threatened to split my head with some crockery
if I didn't stop my infernal warbling.

Later Allah fell into my loins
but propriety prohibits me
  from telling you what happened then.
Let us only say that my wife was pleased,
  and did not threaten me with crockery.

Yesterday, Allah fell into the sky
and it lit up like fire.
It moved my soul to wonder.

This morning, Allah has fallen into my tea
and the pleasure I experience as I hold it on my tongue
is pure religion.

Real Lovers

I am tired of being henpecked
by well-meaning but wrongheaded people
who seem to think it's their responsibility
to make sure I am doing my religion "right."

Apparently, there is a rule book somewhere
   that dictates the proper behavior in every situation,
lists acceptable language,
   and hints at those words that are prohibited
   (for it would never come right out and say them),
and provides a comprehensive guide
   to not scandalizing the community.

No one has ever been so kind
   as to ever give me a copy of this book, though.
It is not the Qu'ran,
   for it actually contains much that these people object to.
It is not the Hadith, for I have read most of them
and I don't think the Prophet—peace be upon him—
would have passed muster with these folks.

Listen to Najat: if anyone ever *did* give me such a book,
I think I would use it for kindling.
Religion that is orderly and seemly
is built upon a nostalgia for passion long spent.

Real lovers are always getting into trouble.

Religion

I realize that there are some who whisper against me
over their tea in the shops, saying,
"That Sufi is against religion"

…which is absurd. I love my religion.
I just don't think it ought to be confused
with the Truth.

Be not quick to condemn Najat
until he has explained himself,
please.

The mind of Allah is vast.
If you think you can comprehend it,
your sin is pride.

If you think the Prophet could comprehend it
—peace be upon him—you make him more than a man,
and therefore you are a heretic.

Islam is like a vast but circumscribed sea.
It is shallow enough that fools can bathe in it but not drown.
It is deep enough that scholars will never exhaust its treasures.

And yet, as the fishermen of Ephesus know of their sea,
it is so full of life that it can sustain all,
none will go to bed hungry—not this night, not any.

It is therefore the greatest of treasures,
our life, and the greatest of gifts
from the hand of Allah.

And yet, this sea is contained by a shore,
for if it covered the whole of the earth
there would be no place for people.

Islam describes the world, but it is not itself the world.
Islam teaches us how to live, but it is not the breath of life.
Islam teaches us wisdom,
  but it does not exhaust the mind of Allah.

Our religion is great.
The Prophet was great.
But Allah is greater.

God is great!
God is great!
Now tell me I am against religion.

Responsibility

I am not sure what you want from me.
I cannot drink this water for you.
I cannot chew your food.

I cannot relieve myself on your behalf,
nor can I study to your benefit.
My going to the doctor will not make you well.

I am not being cruel,
I am just telling you the truth.
There are things you must do for yourself.

I can pray until the world ends, but you will not benefit by it.
I can intercede with Allah, but it will bring you no closer to Him.
I can scale the heights of mystic awareness
   but it will not enlighten you even a little bit.

I'm sorry if I seem impatient, but this is simply the way it is.
If you want to grow your soul,
you have to do your own hard work.

So when I say, "Have you prayed?" and you say, "No,"
what am I to think? Other than
this is not something you really want.

A strong man's muscles do not grow big in a day,
but result from long hours of effort,
over many weeks, months, and years.

A wise man does not gain his wisdom
because a jinn poured it into his ear as he slept,
but from a lifetime of observation and study.

It is the same with the soul.
Najat knows this is not what you want to hear,
but sometimes it is kind to say the hard thing.

There is no easy way around this,
and no one can do it for you.
If you will not lift, you cannot ascend.

The Robber

My love covers me like a coat.
He keeps me warm in winter
and shades my skin from the sun.

Last year as I was going home late at night
a man put a knife in my ribs
and told me to give him my coat.

I am not an idiot.
I gave it to him straight away.
To tell you the truth, I haven't missed it.

If anyone should ever demand it,
I would hand over my Love just as fast.
You wouldn't even have to threaten me.

Although my Beloved is mine
He does not belong to me.
I wish I could give Him away to everyone.

Najat says, If a robber would put my Beloved on like a coat
the only thing he would ever need to steal again
are kisses.

The Rules of Propriety

I know my lovesick madness confuses you.
You do not understand why a grown man
would run into a garden longing to roll in flowers,
why tears stream from his face as he gazes at the stars,
why he would spin around until he topples over,
why he would sing nonsense rhymes to the cows,
why he would go into fits of ecstasy
  at the sound of the muezzin.

I know that this is not acceptable behavior in society,
this is not how responsible adults behave.
But it should be.

Listen to Najat: The rules of propriety are a dangerous trap.
No one will tell you this, but I will:
they are poisonous to the soul.
And I'll tell you something else, that you will only hear from me:
Allah does not want you on your best behavior.

Save Your Feet

A merchant travelled all the way to China and back
and said that he never once saw any sign of Allah.

Yet my neighbor Amahl,
who has never once visited our neighboring village,
can talk your ear off describing God in the most intimate detail.

When I asked him about this, Amahl laughed and said,
"I do not know if Allah is in China. And really, I do not care.
All I know is that there are two of us sharing this house."
Before Amahl's wife died last year, there were three.

Najat says, save your feet, for the beloved is not a foreigner.
And do not strain your eyes looking for Allah.

Eyes are not the only organs that see.

Sickness

Today, I am making soup
because Tajit, the new imam
is coughing his head off and rolling on his mat at home.

You might wonder that I, a dervish,
would be concerned for the imam,
but that is because you don't understand me.

I love our imams, I really do.
Unlike the widows, though, I don't believe
they can fly to Jerusalem on winged horses over night.

They are just men, like myself.
They struggle with the same desires,
and wrestle against the same nafs.

They fail just as regularly,
sin just as badly
speak just as foolishly as any of the rest of us.

Let the widows praise them in voices that rival the muezzin,
and let the merchants dismiss them as hypocrites,
but Najat knows the truth about imams:

Sin is a sickness
that sweeps through every village as regularly as rain in winter.
Even the imams catch cold now and again.

Silence

I notice that there has been a great deal of silence
between Allah and you of late.
There are two kinds of silence.

In one kind, you are faced away from your Beloved.
You have closed off your heart,
  you have stopped speaking—and listening—
and have spurned all intimate congress between you.

This kind of silence is cold and dead and forbidding.

In the other kind, you are facing towards your Beloved.
Your eyes are fixed on His
  and love radiates between you, filling your heart
and communicating intimacies too tender for words.

This kind of silence begat the worlds.

I do not presume to know what is happening
between you and Allah, so perhaps you will tell me.
Which way are you facing?

Silly Chatter

I pray a little here and a little there, all day long.
But most of my prayer is of little importance.
In fact, most of it is just chatter.

I sing silly songs to my Beloved,
gossip about the people I care about most,
and engage in inane pillow talk.

Do you think prayer must always be serious?
Do you think my time of communion with Allah is solemn?
Do you think I come before the Lord of Heaven
  with anything less than reverence?

Prayer is the silly chatter between friends.
I would rather risk offending the Beloved
than boring Him.

Speak

I know that someone hurt you.
I can see it in your eyes
when the muezzin sounds.

You bow, you kneel, you prostrate yourself
your mouth moves with the words of the prayers.
Your body prays, but it is clear to me that your heart does not.

Come to my rooms.
Sit here, allow me to pour you some tea.
Let us talk.

Anything you say in this place is safe
from widow's talk or the wrath of zealots.
There is no one here but us two bumbling seekers.

Even Allah will respect your privacy,
and will drive away the jinn
so that the only ears that hear your words will be mine.

Nothing you can say will surprise me.
You can utter no heresy that I have not heard before.
You cannot truly blaspheme if you are only being honest.

Perhaps the imams have betrayed you.
If so, tell me that story.
The imams are often wrong, and some are even cruel.

Perhaps Allah has abandoned you. That story, too,
you can tell in safety. When you are ready,
I will stand beside you as you confront Him with His offenses.

Don't look at me like that.
Allah is a powerful God, and can weather any abuse
you can level at Him.

Ah, I can see it in your eyes
that you are afraid of Hell
if you dare speak to Allah in this way.

Allow Najat to comfort you.
I speak to Allah this way all the time.
All lovers fight.

If there is no honesty, no redress, no accountability,
there is no relationship. Allah wants nothing from you
quite so much as relationship.

I know you are scared, but my friend, you must speak
   of the barrier that separates you and Allah.
Once you have named it, together we can overcome it.

So speak! Speak! Whatever is weighing down your soul.
For if you are not free to speak your mind
you are not free to love.

Spiritual Master

Today a dervish showed up at my house,
bowed before me and announced that he would
study at the feet of a master if only I would have him.

So I cuffed his ears and threw him into the street.
It was the only merciful thing to do.
If people think I am some kind of spiritual master,
  someone is bound to get hurt.

I will only disappoint them
and my reputation may never recover.
Best to send him packing early.

"Spiritual master," he said. Who is he kidding?
Not me. Not Allah. Not you, if you know me at all.
Only himself. Let him delude himself at someone else's feet.

I am no spiritual master.
I have achieved no state of enlightenment
nor any stage of advanced spiritual understanding.

I am neither prophet, seer, nor adept.
I'll tell you what I *have* learned, however,
and perhaps that will serve to instruct you.

I have learned to love Allah with my whole heart
and I have learned how to fight with Him fair and square.
What more does anyone need to know, really?

Spiritual Progress

It sometimes feels that my path towards Allah
is an arduous climb
scrambling for footholds,
precarious and exhausting.

But in truth, I think this is my own imagination at work
because when I pray
it does not seem as though I am speaking from below
but beholding all creation spread out before me
a gift given to me alone by the Ruler of All.

Spiritual progress isn't made by hauling oneself
  hand over hand towards some imagined summit
but allowing oneself to fall
  into arms that cannot fail to catch you
because there is no object in all of creation
  dearer to Allah than your soul.

If you dismiss everything I have ever said,
hear what Najat says now:
Allah does not want your effort
but only your letting go.

Stray Dog

A stray dog is driving me crazy
following me everywhere I go.

Her too-cute mangy face pops up
  every time I go out onto the street,
and she waits for me every time I enter a doorway,
head on her paws, whimpering.

What am I going to do with her?

Halfway through my day I think,
"I am like this dog, tagging along after Allah,
whining for Him whenever He disappears."

I feel proud.

Big mistake. My soul speaks to me, saying,
"Najat, you fool, you flatter yourself too much.
You are nowhere near as faithful as that dog."

Then I think, Of course! The dog is Allah,
chasing after me everywhere I go, shadowing my every step
whining for my attention.

I feel special.

Big mistake. My soul speaks to me again, saying,
"Najat, you fool, you flatter yourself too much.
Allah has better things to do than follow you around all day."

I scowl at the dog.
She wags her tail and gives a little jump.
I touch her fur, she licks at my hand.

I am just Najat. This dog is just a dog.
Can I not love her without turning her into something else?
Apparently not. Never mind the dog,
  the religious imagination is the tenacious bitch.

Submitting All Things

Last night I asked my wife
if she had submitted in all things
to the will of Allah

whereupon she loudly announced
that submission to me was quite arduous enough
and that no reasonable deity could possibly require more.

I was shaken by this pronouncement
and it caused me to reflect upon
how much wiser than myself my wife often is.

Starting tomorrow I shall begin a new spiritual discipline:
I shall submit in all things, spiritual and temporal,
to my wife

and I trust that Allah
will marvel
at my new scrupulosity.

Sufism

Sufism is not a religion.
It is the living, beating heart of faith,
regardless of what religion you happen to be.

Other People of the Book have Sufis,
although since they speak other languages
they have other words for them.

Religion is the husk surrounding the grain.
Living faith is the meat it protects,
like a shining pearl in its shell.

Religion is the container, the clothes, the form
that contains and provides a vehicle for
a living faith that cannot be spoken, or written down.

Do not, O Muslim, confuse Islam with living faith.
Yet living faith cannot survive without Islam,
nor can Islam survive without living faith.

But they are not the same. The practice of Islam
leads either to the soul's entombment or its liberation.
Whether living faith is present will determine its destiny.

Sufis do not seek to form a religion
  —we already have a fine one.
We seek only to set Islam on fire by igniting its heart.
We seek only to make it live.

Sunni and Shia

There is an old Shia woman who carries water in our village,
and every time she passes the well
the women spit on her.

It makes me sad. It makes Allah sad as well.
There is enough sadness here between Sunni and Shia
to fill that well a thousand times over.

I know the imams will say that I am wrong
and perhaps even blasphemous for saying this,
but say it I must.

It is not better to be Sunni than to be Shia.
It is not better to be Shia than to be Sunni.

Sin has seeped into every jar,
and all are equally tainted.

But love can be found in every jar as well,
mixed up inseparably with that sin.

All of us have drunk it.
All of us suffer.
All of us benefit.

Najat says, Allah sees no difference
between Sunni and Shia.
He only sees people who are equally thirsty
and have only unclean water to drink.

Surrender

I understand if you do not want to abandon yourself to Allah.

He is, after all, almighty, and you are weak.
He is, after all, omniscient, and you know so little.
He is, after all, omnipresent,
   and you can only be... wherever you are.

Surrender to such a being is a frightening prospect
—but I strongly recommend that you do it.

Because if you are suffering under the illusion
that you are strong, wise,
   or master of more land than you are standing on
you need to be taken down a notch or two.

Najat knows just how to do it:

Put your ass in the air
five times a day
in front of your women and children and servants.

The Prophet—peace be upon him—knew what he was doing.
The heart must be humbled
   before it can know true strength, wisdom, or power.
Only if you surrender your pride
will Allah give you what you really desire in its place.

Talk and Listen

When I ask students about prayer,
all of them know how to bow towards Mecca.
This is the Prayer of the Body, and it is important.

But when I ask them about the Prayer of the Heart,
some of them have no idea what I am talking about.
These are the easy cases. They have little to unlearn.

Others, though, say that they talk to Allah
all day and all night. And I think, "my poor, poor Beloved
—who can bear to hear such incessant chatter?"

Still others say that they wait in silence
for the Beloved's voice. And sometimes
they even hear it.

There is nothing wrong with the chatterers
    or the lovers of silence,
not really. Both of them are necessary.
The trouble comes when a seeker does only one
    and not the other.

Every wife wants her husband to talk.
Every wife wants her husband to listen.
Every husband hates to do either, usually.

But the wife knows what makes a good relationship.
It is this kind of relationship Allah wants to have
with each and every person alive.

So, my dear ones, listen to Najat:
if you want to be healed, talk.
if you want to be wise, listen.

But if you want to know the deepest intimacy
with your Beloved,
you must learn to do both.

The Teacher's Wisdom

You come to me, and you call me "teacher."
I make you tea and call you "friend."
We kneel with focused attention before Allah
   and we call it "prayer."

Don't look to me for answers. Don't suppose for a minute
that I know what I'm doing, here. I don't.
It isn't my wisdom being spoken into the silence between us.

I open my mouth and the winds of heaven
   move my lips, or they don't.
When we are finished, we will be fortunate
   if we are both a little wiser.

I am not the teacher. I am the tea-maker.
Allah is the teacher.
You and I are both students, and always will be.

My Love, if I ever get to the point where I say,
   "I can answer that"
please do not strike me dead.
But kindly persuade my wife to inform me
   that my teaching days are over.

For if I think I have any answers,
if I am foolish enough to believe that I know what I am doing,
if I am ever arrogant enough to suppose
   that my own wisdom exceeds yours,

then my usefulness in this world is at an end
and my time is better spent wetting myself
  and drooling into a towel
until the angel of sleep closes my eyes forever to this good life.

Najat is only skilled as a teacher
by knowing that his own wisdom is only slightly more valuable
than his excrement.

Tease

On this day when my heart feels like sand
and words fail me
my Love leans in to offer His lips
but mine meet nothing but the air.

You tease!

The Third Way

You wouldn't go to a chicken for milk,
unless you are demented.
Just so, you should not go to Najat for a fatwa.

A chisel is a useful tool, unless you need to hammer a nail.
Then, it is just awkward.
Just so, if what you want is a ruling on jurisprudence,
   Najat is the wrong man for the job.

I am not an imam (Allah be thanked).
I am not a scholar (dogs will chase their tails).
I am a dervish (my chest relaxes and I sigh).

There are three ways that a person can be faithful to Allah,
three ways that the soul can find its way
and the first two are easy:

You can do the right things
—the imams will be happy to tell you
   what those are and how to do them
You can believe the right things
—the scholars will let you know
   when they've reached a consensus.

But the third way is hard,
and requires much close listening, discernment, and effort
on the part of any who pursue it.

The third way is to do what is beautiful,
to love what you love,
to sing the songs that demand singing,
to express what cannot be spoken,
except in the language of the heart.

If you want to know how to do that,
you have come to the right place,
and Najat is your man.

This Silence is Pregnant

This silence is pregnant
with Vision
gathering itself
to pounce upon your brain
if you will just shut up
and sit still
long enough
to let it land on you.

Göreme, Cappadocia, Turkey

Today's Inspiration

Today my inspiration comes
not from the Prophet—peace be upon him—
nor from the flashes of revelation
that often descend upon me
when I am caught up in Allah's embrace.

Today my inspiration comes
not from my daily prostrations toward Mecca
nor—as it so often does—in sharing with the poor
or contemplating the insights of the dervish poets.

No. Today, I have been inspired
by the fierce regularity of creation
by the steady beat of my blood
by the waxing of the moon
by the dependability of the sun
by the tenacity of springtime.

Here, a mosquito has landed on Najat's arm.
I know it will bite me, and such knowledge
fills my heart and makes me glad.

Too Much

There have been too many harsh words of late,
too much rushing about, too much to be done
—too much, too much, too much.

This night let soft rain falling on leaves
be the only sound in our ears
This night let the gentle pull of the ground win out.

This night let there be just enough to actually enjoy:
your arm around my belly, pulling me in close,
your breath warming the back of my neck.

This night let there be a word or two whispered every hour,
but only when needed.
Most times, a nuzzle is enough.

I could die this way, and be content.
And when the time comes,
I think I will.

Tragedies

I call these petty inconveniences in my life "tragedies,"
but you and I both know how selfish,
self-centered, and just plain crazy that is.

These are not tragedies.
They are the fist of Allah
  pounding away at the door of my heart,
smashing everything I have invested in
  that is not Him.

They are the hammer of Abraham,
smashing the idols in the Kabah
to the horror of his father and the villagers.

Indeed, I must be grateful for them,
for they are the only thing standing between me
and the delusion that I am alone sufficient for all of my needs.

In truth, I hate trouble as much as you do.
It takes faith to see the hand of Allah in it.
Submission, O Muslims, takes a lifetime!

So today I will submit even my resentment
at being inconvenienced.
And tomorrow I will be given the opportunity
  to submit again.

Two Kinds of People

There are two kinds of people in the world.
There are those who have learned how to love
and those who are still learning.

Those who have mastered the art of love we call "prophets"
—peace be upon them—and they are our teachers
Ibrahim, Isma'il, Dawud, Sulayman, Musa, Isa, Muhammad...
  and many others.

All the rest of us are learning.

Listen to Najat: There really is an "us" and "them"
but it has nothing to do with borders or race or religion.

It has only to do with
whether you know
when you are being kissed.

Göreme, Cappadocia, Turkey

Vision

Oh, dear. I know that look.
Allah has come upon you.
Do come and sit down before you topple over
   and hurt someone.

Drink this tea.
Catch your breath.
And tell me what happened.

I remember when it last happened to me.
I was at the well, getting a drink of water.
And Allah fell upon me like a cat pouncing from a roof top,
   claws extended to clutch at my shoulder.

It was all I could do to remain upright.
My brain felt like it was on fire,
and I saw reflected in the well all of the worlds
   and their myriad creatures.

I was lucky I didn't fall in.
And yet, in a way, I did fall in.
I fell into the mind of Allah, and I will never be the same.

It has happened before, don't misunderstand,
but every time is different.
Every time you see something new that you did not see before.

And every time it illumines all that is shadow,
exposes everything that is a lie
and turns me once again to face Mecca in my heart.

I do not know why Allah does this to people
and you can never predict when it happens.
My advice is to see it as a blessing
   rather than the uncomfortable imposition it feels like now.

But Najat does know one thing:
once it has happened to you, you will sell everything
—even your soul—to make sure it happens again.

We Are All Broken

Have you fallen, and broken?
Do you fear that no one can love you in such a sorry state?

We are all broken.
Some try to hide it,
some try to pretend it never happened,
some are ashamed and lash out
  at anyone who gets too close to the wound.

Najat says, come to the café,
order some coffee, and sit among friends.
You will find that not a single person who drinks with us
  lacks a scar.
We will compare them
and laugh about how we got that way.

Wake Up

Your soul and my soul are not different things.
We behold the same glory through windows
that we either clean, or we don't.

Your soul and Allah are not different things.
His glory is yours,
so how ready are you to shine?

This entire world radiates from the blazing heart of Allah.
Every creature is a revelation of the glory of God,
And testifies to His faithfulness and mercy.

Every moment we live
is the cry of the muezzin, calling all to prayer.
Every action is a prostration.

If you don't live like this,
You have forgotten who you are.
Najat's teaching is your coffee. Wake up!

Weak Words

My imam and your mother
both seem convinced
that a sufficient quantity of words
can make and sustain their worlds.

My heart goes out to them.
I do not stop them from trying
but words are simply not strong enough
to pull the weight that these kind people require.

They are like hand baskets
in which they are attempting to carry camels.
The baskets always snap and it irritates the camels.
No one likes irritated camels.

Listen to Najat's words, now:
Stop talking. Trust the silence.
This is what makes the world
and sustains it.

What Allah is Feeling

I have just come from the Mosque, and I am shaking my head
I do not understand where the Imam gets his information.

If you listened only to Him, and not to your heart
you would think that Allah spends most of his time angry
—at sinners, at heretics, at infidels, and especially at Sufis.

But I talk to Allah frequently,
and anger is not what I hear from Him.

I hear his deep sighing
  for those who do not return his amorous advances.
I hear Him desperate to be loved, talking constantly,
like a girl with a crush when everyone but she
  knows it is hopeless.

I hear Him worrying about people until I am sick of hearing it
and threaten to throw Him out with the old tea
if He does not stop his mooning.

There's no reasoning with Him.
I talk, He sighs. I pour more tea. He paces.
I try to change the subject, He walks out into the night
without even grabbing His hat.

Najat says: I don't know. Maybe He is angry. I would be.
But the emotion I hear most from Allah
is longing, and a deep and aching sadness.

What Allah is Like

If you ask people what Allah is like
it can tell you much about whether
    they are in a state of submission
or whether they are fighting with all that they have
in quiet ways or loud
to keep Allah safely at a distance.

If a person sees Allah as a blazing sun,
seeing all and having mercy on none,
you can bet this person tries to protect himself,
    and will often stay indoors.

If a person sees Allah as a father,
always giving advice and protective,
she will try to get away with anything, and hope she isn't seen.

If a person sees Allah as a light,
piercing all darkness and illuminating the world
he will live in shame of the shadow in his own soul.

If a person sees Allah as a schoolmaster,
expecting studiousness and discipline,
she will be fatigued and resentful.

This is why the Prophet—peace be upon him—
prohibited the use of images.
They are all inadequate, and they invariably lie.

I don't think Allah is *like* anything.
Allah is like nothing else in Heaven and earth.
If that scares you, you are wise.

You protest: "But you are constantly saying
  that Allah is like a lover."
But my friend, if you will remember carefully,
  you'll find you are mistaken.
I have never said Allah is *like* a lover,
but that Allah *is* a lover,
and more: Allah is Love.

Listen to Najat: Don't try to figure Allah out.
The ninety-nine names* will only lead you astray.
Just give up every image, every idea, every conception.
Submit, prostrate your body and your mind,
  and let yourself be loved.

*An Islamic tradition names ninety-nine names, or attributes, of Allah.

What Islam is About

Yesterday I drank tea with a man
who said he understood everything
about the Prophet—peace be upon him.

When I asked him to explain the Prophet to me
he told me that the Prophet was all about Paradise
and that nothing on this earth was of any value.

I smiled and drank the man's coffee
and politely did not inform him
that he was an idiot.

The Prophet—peace be upon him—believed in Heaven,
as assuredly as we all do, for the Revelation is clear on this.
But his concern was not for Heaven.

His concern was for the relentless cycle
  of bloodshed and revenge
that ravaged his people.
His concern was for the widows and orphans that went hungry
while fat men feasted on oxen and grouse.

His concern was to stop the violence
that unchecked pride wrecks upon a village
and erect in its place a Law answerable to justice and love.

That is what Islam is about.
If you want to chase daydreams about Heaven
that's your affair. But don't bring the Prophet into it.

Listen to Najat: Allah is not to be found in the sky
or in the afterlife of your fantasies.
Allah is found when you kiss the dust
and surrender all that you have
to another.

What Prayer is For

Whenever the muezzin sounds his call,
people all face towards Mecca and fall on their faces.
But if you ask them what prayer is *for*
they look at you as if you are trying to trick them.

Listen, my friends, no one is trying to trick you.
But in my opinion, while the imams have done a very good job
explaining *how* we should pray,
they have not done a very good job at explaining *why*.

Prayer is not designed to change the mind of Allah
  —what hubris!
Prayer is not commanded in order to instruct Allah
  —Allah alone knows all!
Prayer does not effect change in the outside world
  —your will is so strong only in your dreams!

Prayer is only this—to share your life with Allah,
to open to Him the feelings of your heart
and the concerns of your mind,

to enjoy His presence and to be still long enough
  so that He may hold you and rock you
as your mother used to do on those long ago nights
when the moon threatened
  to crash through your bedroom window.

Listen to Najat. Why should you pray?
Because the moon is big, *now*.

What They Do Not Teach

I've studied in the madrasahs.
I know what they teach, there.
Admirable stuff, some of it:

I like the theology, I love the rhetoric.
History can be useful, poetry is ecstatic,
although I can take or leave the jurisprudence.

And no imam is worth his weight in hummus
if he doesn't know the Qu'ran well enough
to produce a competent fatwa.

But it makes me sad to think of all of the
things absolutely necessary for the health of the soul
that they will never hear within those walls.

They do not teach you how to listen
for the mooning cry of the Beloved
heard only late at night when the heart is silent.

They do not teach you how to return Allah's advances
or how to do the dance of courtship
that draws lovers together in their hearts.

They do not teach you how to roll passionately
in the arms of the Beloved
intermingling body and spirit until two are one.

And as far as Najat is concerned,
these things they do not teach
are all you *really* need to know about religion.

Göreme, Cappadocia, Turkey

What They Say About You

You must know what they say about you:
you have lost your mind,
you are immoral,
you are a heretic and worthy of death.
I don't know if these things are true.
Probably.
But they say these things about me as well, you see,
and about everyone who has ever truly found Love.

Najat says, Be easy.
It's jealousy that causes them to gossip.
Those envious wags
aren't half as mad or wanton or heathen as we are.
Not in their wildest dreams.

What You Were Made For

Poverty is hard, it is a strain upon the soul
for it causes people to do shameful things
that they otherwise would not.

Wealth is harder, it damns the soul
for it causes people to do shameful things
even when they don't have to do them.

I have known good people who were poor.
I have known good people who were rich
—though not as many.
To walk either path with integrity is a calling that few possess.

Certainly I am not one of them.
This clot that is me was not formed by Allah
for such a precarious vocation.
And unless I miss my guess, you weren't, either.

You were made to hear and recognize
the voice calling out to you
from beyond the desert of your own concerns.

You were made for tenderness,
for gentle correction when you stray
and extravagant praise when you shine.

You were made to be held close
to that breast that gives suck to the world,
giving you warmth and sustenance and salvation.

Najat is no idiot. Money is dangerous,
   and few of us do it well.
But love is safe, its Voice is clear,
   its embrace is wide
and everyone, everyone, everyone is called
   to come and snuggle.

When A Person Falls in Love

When a person falls in love,
she expresses it in one of two ways.
Either she shouts it from the rooftops,
so that all the world will share in her joy,
or she holds it like a secret in her heart
admiring it like stolen jewelry when no one else is around.

Najat does not shout his love from the rooftops,
for that is the way one ends up in prison.
Instead, he *pretends* his love is a secret,
but he whispers about it to *everyone*.

When You Finally Submit

When you finally submit,
when you finally consent to be intimate with the Beloved
and enter into His bedchamber
you share everything that is yours with Him.

You empty from your satchel
all that you have been carrying around:
All of your hurt, your joy,
your anger, your contentments,
your confusion, your loves,
your fears, your hopes.

You lay it all before Him,
discussing each thing,
laughing over the shiny items,
crying together over those that are broken.

When you are finished and the silence has quieted your soul
the Beloved takes his turn
and shares everything that is His with you.

He gives to you salvation and strength,
wisdom and comfort
discernment and love
… and that's just for starters.

When two people become one,
their possessions are united as well.
In this union with the Beloved,
Najat knows who got the better end of the deal.

Who Am I?

We are told that Allah has forbidden wine to the faithful
yet when the Beloved's own cupbearer brings me a full chalice,
who am I to refuse?

We are told that Allah requires prayers five times a day.
Yet, if I am so enthralled in my ecstacy,
  beholding the Beloved in my heart
that I forget to bow toward Mecca, am I at fault?

We are told that we must keep only to our wives,
that any other dalliance is fornication and will lead to Hell.
But when the Beloved beckons me with that come-hither gaze,
  chastity is impossible.

I have tried to be a good Muslim. Really, I have.
But in my heart, I am much more interested
in being a good lover.

Who I Am

This family is who I am.
It's not the only family to be a part of, certainly.
It is not better than any other family.
But it's *my* family, and I love them.

This path is who I am.
It's not the only path.
It is not better than any other path.
But it's *my* path, and so I walk it with joy.

This religion is who I am.
It's not the only religion.
It is not better than any other religion.
But it's *my* religion, and so I practice it with reverence.

I am not alone. There are others on this journey.
I have family members, traveling companions,
    brothers and sisters of the Ummah
who make my life rich, meaningful, and valuable.

Najat knows who he is.
And he knows he is nothing without others.
Allah, in His wisdom, made us for community.

Who Needs the Mosque?

Today I met a man who admitted
—with darting eyes and a hushed tone—
that he never goes to the mosque.

He never hears the recitation of the Holy Qu'ran,
never listens to the Imam's sermons,
never gives alms.

He says he can worship Allah just fine
  spending the day praying in the desert.
I asked him when the last time
  he spent a day praying in the desert was.
He looked like he wanted to punch me.

Look, I get it. The mosque is filled with hypocrites,
—I am one of them, so I should know.
And the Imam isn't the best preacher I've ever heard.

But it's hard to build the Ummah—the Just Society
if you're always ducking actual people.
It's the pains in the ass, after all, that grow your soul.

Listen to Najat:
Sure, it's possible to grow spiritually all by yourself,
  but it'll take you a lot longer to do it.
A three-legged dog can certainly cover some ground,
  but it still only has three legs.

Who Told You?

Who told you that this world is a sad and dangerous place?
Who told you that people were untrustworthy and corrupt?
Who told you that you were worthless and stupid?

I think you were set up.
Tell someone a story about a jinn and guess what?
They see jinn everywhere.

Listen to Najat as he tells you another story:

This world is an oasis, teeming with life and joy.
Everywhere you go you will find people
   who are caring and responsible.
And you are a treasure beyond price
   ... and smart enough to see it.

Whoever told you those things,
you should find them,
you should wrap your arms around them,
hold them close,
and tell them
that Allah has a special place in Hell for liars.

Why Should I Pray?

Spiritual seekers always ask me the same question,
"Why should I pray?
Doesn't God already know what I need?"

This is a question for religious people, not for lovers.
Lovers do not need to ask why they should crack jokes,
whisper pillow talk, worry aloud, or make love.

Praying isn't a list of things you want from the market,
it's the kind of proposition best accompanied
by slowly rolling your tongue over your lips,
  and the batting of bedroom eyes.

Najat says, face Mecca and prostrate yourself five times a day.
Making love is easier lying down, anyway.

You Must Move

Allah is like a hawk,
his eyes are drawn to motion.
If you don't want Him to notice you, do nothing.

If, however, you crave His attention,
if you long for His caresses and His care,
you must move.

You must laugh like an idiot,
dance like a bridegroom,
and sing like a sparrow.

It isn't piety that will make you irresistible to Allah,
it's the irrepressible joy found
in simply living your life.

So sing loudly, dance wildly, speak boldly
love wantonly, give generously, pray sincerely
work hard, hug tight, kiss wet.

There's nothing to be gained
from being small.
God is great—you go and be great, too.

Your Piety

I have seen you pray in the marketplace
at unprescribed times where everyone will see you.
What are you trying to accomplish?

You might gain a reputation for holiness amongst the widows,
But trust me, my friend,
Allah cares nothing for your piety.

Your prayers do not move Him,
your almsgiving does not impress Him,
your pilgrimage wins you no merit in Heaven.

I think you are wasting your time.
So, why, you might ask, did the Prophet
—peace be upon him—command us to practice?

Not to win Allah's favor,
nor to bolster your dubious reputation
amongst the village folk.

We are commanded to pray, give alms, and go to Mecca
for one reason and one reason only:
to batter down the doors of your stubborn pride.

If you use these things to reinforce those doors,
you are lost.

Listen to Najat, for he will tell you something
that the Imams will never admit.
Allah is only impressed by your willingness to be broken.

The Spice Market, Istanbul.

Your Wealth is Not Yours

Stop. Just stop and look at yourself.
Look at what you're doing, what you're saying,
what an ungrateful boor you've become.

You do not own your home,
your wealth is not yours,
this body does not belong to you.

Your wife is not your property,
your children are not your property.
Your property does not even belong to you,
  regardless of what those dusty papers say.

This is Allah's world.
This is Allah's land.
These are Allah's people.

Your wife belongs to Allah, as do your children.
Your own body, loaned to you by Allah's grace,
will be taken from you one day
  and returned to the ground whence it came.

And yet here you are, strutting like a peacock
and pretending that all you survey is yours.
You are not a wealthy man, but a fool.

Listen to Najat, who owns nothing but wisdom:
You are a wayfarer, a traveler.
You are passing through this world.

You cannot stay.
Any attempt to hold onto any of it will be met with failure,
as your fingers uncurl and turn to dust.

Give glory to Allah, who is a gracious host.
Give praise to Allah, who has lent you comfortable rooms
and provided merry companions for your journey.

Be grateful for His hospitality
and stop pretending that you have a *right* to any of it.
There is nothing worse than an ungrateful guest.

The Secret

Discover the secret about Najat Ozkaya at:
www.apocryphile.org/secret.html

About the Translator

JOHN R. MABRY is professor of interfaith theology and spiritual direction at the Chaplaincy Institute for Arts and Interfaith Ministry in Berkeley, CA, and assistant director of the Master's Program in Interfaith Spiritual Guidance at the Institute of Transpersonal Psychology in Palo Alto. He has served as associate pastor—and later pastor—at Grace North Church (Congregational) for nearly twenty years. He has written numerous books on spirituality, spiritual guidance, and world religions. He sings for two progressive rock bands in the South Bay, Metaphor and Mind Furniture. He lives in Oakland, CA, with his wife and dog.

Visit his website at: www.apocryphile.org/jrm

www.ingramcontent.com/pod-product-compliance
Lightning Source LLC
Chambersburg PA
CBHW080531090426
42733CB00015B/2556